The Night Before Christmas
✦✦✦ The Rest of the Story

A True Story Based on New Testament Scripture

ADELINE OWEN

ISBN 978-1-63575-022-5 (Hard Cover)
ISBN 978-1-63575-021-8 (Digital)

Christian Faith Publishing, Inc.
296 Chestnut Street
Meadville, PA 16335
www.christianfaithpublishing.com

Printed in the United States of America

To my family:

My husband, Todd, for praying with
and for me about everything;

Our daughter, Hannah, and her husband, Adam;

Our daughter, Laura, and her husband, Andrew;

Our son, Tyler;

Our extended family, church family, and friends,
You have all given me such wonderful
love, help, and support!

Most of all,

To my Lord God, Who is the reason for this book!

May all the glory go to Him!

On the night before Christmas in Bethlehem town,
All the people were busy and rushing around;

They had come to be counted and taxed in that day;
Young Joseph and Mary came a long way to pay!

The inns were all full, with no room to spare,
No thought of the Savior that soon would be there.

4

Soon the travelers were cozy, all tucked in their beds,
While Mary and Joseph had concerns in their heads;

With Mary's discomfort and Joseph aware,
They could not settle in! Soon a child would be there!

When through the wee hours, the Baby was born,
There was no one around on that first Christmas morn!

It was Jesus, the Savior, Who was born in that stall,
People hearing God's prophets should've known of it all.

He was born in a stable with straw for His bed,
And Mary and Joseph to cradle His head.

When out in the fields, there appeared such a light,
Shepherds sprang to their feet; they were shaking with fright!

The angels on high were an awesome sight!
They gave out a message and sang through the night;

"Glory to God," were the words that they sang,
"Glory … in the highest," as all the heavens rang.[1]

For to you is born on this very day,
A Savior in Bethlehem; you'll find Him on the hay.

---

[1] Direct quotes from NIV Bible. Luke 2:14

Angels went back to heaven; the shepherds then said,
"Let us go now to Bethlehem," so they went on ahead;[2]

Away to that city, they took off like a flash,
Shepherds were the only ones making the dash.

The moon and the stars o'r the valley so low,
Shown with brightness of noonday on objects below;

---

[2] Direct quote from the New Revised Standard Version (NRSV) of the Bible.

13

When what to their wondering eyes should they see,
But a Babe in the manger—of a stall—could it be?

This new little Baby, so wondrous and small
Would save the whole world that was ruined by the fall?

The Savior of all had been born on that night,
With no one to welcome Him—God's wondrous light.

They found the new Savior, as angels did say,
They knew that the Lord was revealed on that day;

As they fell to their knees, to worship the King,
They remembered the angels and what they did sing.

The shepherds made known all the things they had seen.
The countrymen wondered what this could mean.

Then back to the fields, to the sheep they did go,
And gave glory to God for the things they now know.

And Mary rejoiced within her own heart,
It had all been amazing, right from the start.

After Jesus was born, when Herod was king,
Wise men came from the East, and gifts they did bring;

They followed the star and rejoiced as they came,
To the place Jesus was, and they worshiped His name;

They presented their gifts to the King from above:
Gold, frankincense, and myrrh, their offerings of love.

Being warned by the Lord in a dream that same night
Not to go back to Herod, a different way, they took flight.

Jesus grew wise and tall; in the Bible we see:
He touched people, healed people; love was the key;

Some of them followed—He showed them the way,
But others just laughed—as they still do today;

He showed them God's love as He taught and forgave;
He wanted them to know that He came, souls to save;

It was God's perfect plan, that is why Jesus came,
To cleanse all from sin, who believe in His name.

But they mocked Him and beat Him! They were cruel as could be!

They did not understand, He came for all, you see.

Then laying aside His very life, He chose
The way of the cross! The third day, He arose!

He was seen by disciples and Mary and others,
They saw Him alive, many sisters and brothers.

He said, "Go (to) the world, and (tell them of Me)."[3]
God the Spirit will help you; just go, you will see.

---

[3] Direct quote from NIV Bible. Mark 16:15

Then suddenly, He was taken up before their own eyes,
In a cloud up to heaven; they stared at the skies.

But we've heard in God's Word, since He rose out of sight,
That He's coming back soon! Are you ready tonight?

God sent His Son, Jesus, to earth to die for our sins so that we don't have to! God's Word says that whoever believes in Jesus will get to live forever with Him in heaven someday!

+ *God loves you so much!*

John 3:16 NIV, "*For God so loved the world* that He gave His one and only Son, that whoever believes in Him shall not perish but have eternal life."

+ *Your sin separates you from God and must be washed away by Jesus in order for you to be right with God!*

Romans 3:23 NIV, "For *all have sinned* and fall short of the glory of God."

Romans 6:23 NIV, "For the wages of sin is death, but the gift of God is eternal life in Christ Jesus our Lord."

Romans 5:8b NIV, "While *we were still sinners,* Christ died for us."

First John 1:9 NIV, "*If we confess our sins,* He is faithful and just and will forgive us our sins and purify us from all unrighteousness."

Second Corinthians 5:21 NIV, "*God made Him who had no sin to be sin for us* so that in Him we might become the righteousness of God."

- *Believe!* God gives us faith to believe in Him!

Ephesians 2:8–9 NIV, "For it is by grace you have been saved, through faith—and this is not from yourselves, *it is the gift of God*—not by works, so that no one can boast."

John 1:12 NIV, "Yet to all who did receive Him, to those who believed in His name, He gave the right to become children of God."

John 3:16 NIV, "For God so loved the world that *He gave His one and only Son, that whoever believes in Him shall not perish but have eternal life.*"

Live and grow in your relationship with God:
- Get involved in a Bible-believing church!
- Read God's Word!
- Pray!

About the Author

Adeline grew up on a farm near Osakis, Minnesota. She loves the Lord God and wants to share His wonderful plan of salvation with all people! She is a teacher and a paraprofessional in her local school district and a Sunday school superintendent at her church. She and her husband, Todd, live in Alexandria, Minnesota, and are blessed with three children and two sons-in-law.

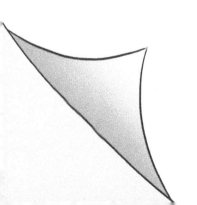

CPSIA information can be obtained
at www.ICGtesting.com
Printed in the USA
BVHW050604051218
534724BV00007B/41/P